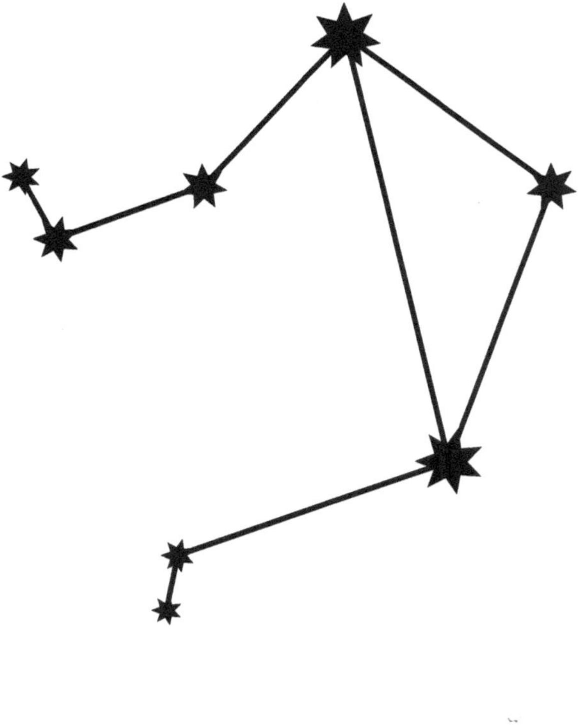

Copyright © 2020 by Heidi Rose Robbins.
Published by One Idea Press Pittsburgh, PA

All rights reserved. No part of this publication may be reproduced, stored in a retrieval system or transmitted in any form or by any means, electronic, mechanical, photocopying, recording or otherwise without the prior permission of the publisher or in accordance with the provisions of the Copyright, Designs and Patents Act 1988 or under the terms of any license permitting limited copying issued by the Copyright Licensing Agency.

For permission requests, write to the publisher, addressed "Attention: Permissions Request," at the following email address: hello@oneideapress.com

Ordering Information:
Quantity sales. Special discounts are available on quantity purchases by corporations, associations, and others. For details, contact the "Special Sales Department" at the following email address: hello@oneideapress.com.

Paperback Edition: 978-1-944134-63-1
Hardback Edition: 978-1-944134-64-8

Printed in the United States of America

Libra

a love letter

Heidi Rose Robbins

with illustrations by
Wyoh Lee

hello love.

(yes, you)

Friends,

I'm so glad you are holding this book! It is filled with encouragement and an ongoing invitation for us all to be more fully who we are.

The best way to work with these books is to purchase one for each of your signs — your Sun, Moon, and Rising Sign.

These are the three most important positions in your astrological chart. You can discover what these are if you enter your exact time, date, and place of birth in any online astrology site. Each position has something unique to offer.

When you read the book for your Moon, think of it as an energy that is very available to you. It's a place where you might feel comfortable. The Moon has to do with our emotional life, our patterns of behavior, and circumstances of our childhood. We can rely on the Moon, but we also want to work to shed the patterns that no longer serve us.

The Sun is our present personality. We can learn a lot about our everyday self in the world. We can learn about the energies we have readily available to us to use in service to our highest calling.

The Rising Sign is the most important point. It is the sign that was rising as we took our first breath. It holds the key to our soul's calling. It is an energy we want to cultivate and be generous with throughout our lives.

So — enjoy the journey. Be sure to read them all!

Welcome
{13}

I. Celebrating Libra
{15}

II. Living Your Libra Love
{61}

III. Growing Your Libra Love
{85}

IV. Questions to Inspire Sharing Your Libra Love
{103}

One Last Little Love Note
{125}

My dear Libra,

This little book is a love letter to your harmonizing, beauty seeking self. It is written to remind you of your many gifts. It is written to be a loving mirror so any page can remind you who you truly are. Take it in, dear Libra. Take your time. Breathe in the bounty you are. Promise me you'll take the time to see your peaceful but passionate self in these pages.

This little book will also explore those places in ourselves that start to close when we want to open, the part of us that hesitates when we want to act. We all have our quirks and difficulties, after all. But if we return again and again to our potency, vulnerability, and sense of possibility, we can outgrow our closures one by one.

Think of this book as a treasure chest containing the golden coins of YOU. Open it when you wish to remember your beauty, worth or great potential. And remember, too, this Libra part of you is just one voice in the symphony of YOU. It cannot possibly contain your complexity and bounty. But it can begin to name just a few of your gifts.

Read this out loud when you can. Read this in the morning. Read it before bed. Read it when you need encouragement. Read it even if you are already feeling peaceful and balanced. Let it fuel you. Read it and own it! Use it and claim it! This is your love letter, Libra. This is the song of YOU.

Big love,
Heidi Rose

Celebrating Libra

As you read this celebration, you will sometimes say "Yes, yes, yes! This is me!" And you may likewise sometimes feel that you have not yet lived into some of these qualities. This is honoring and celebrating the very best of your Libra energy. This is naming the full, conscious, awakened use of your Libra gifts. We are sounding the note of THE POSSIBLE. So, even if you feel you still have work to do in certain areas — as do we all — let these words be inspiration to offer your best Self!

You harmonize.

Dear Libra, you know how to blend and harmonize. You take two seemingly disparate arguments and you find the common ground. You are an agent of understanding.

♎

You are a true diplomat.

You bridge conflicts, dear Libra. You initiate peace. You offer peaceful communication and inspire that in others. You listen patiently and speak to inspire a common good. You bring people, countries, and teams together.

You have an eye for beauty.

You see and name the beautiful, dear Libra. And you often point out the beauty to elevate conversation or cooperation. Beauty is a path towards peace. You know that when something is beautiful, it is inviting. And when we feel invited, we feel received.

♎

You choose the next balanced step.

Though you often weigh things for some time, Libra, when you choose the next right step, you choose with care. You are not rash in your decisions. You initiate with clarity and poise.

You choose the path of peace.

Libra is one of the great signs of peace. And you, Libra, are here to create, stand for, and act on behalf of peace. Make no mistake. Achieving peace is a dynamic process filled with struggle and intensity. And once peace is "achieved," it is not fixed. You strive to keep the peace.

You fight for the right relationship.

It is deeply important for you to speak up for how we treat one another. You stand for equality. You advocate for the necessity to see one another as souls.

You stand for what is fair and just.

There's a good reason that Libra rules the Law. You are an initiator of what is fair and just. You come forth to fight for justice. Fairness is a big theme for you.

♎

You cooperate and initiate cooperation.

You love to work together. Anything we can do alone, you say, is much more fun and productive in collaboration. You love a good partner. You love to give and receive reflection. You are motivated by the give and take.

You wisely pause before your next big leap.

You like to assess. And that will often pay off. You weigh all your options. And you do not rush. Then, when you leap, you are really ready to leap!

♎︎

You have excellent taste.

Venus is one of your ruling planets, dear Libra. And Venus is the planet of beauty. You love what is refined and gorgeous. Whether it be food, or your home or the clothing you wear, you seek out beauty and excellence.

♎

You support the arts.

You believe in culture. When a society lacks culture, it also lacks compassion, love and decency. You know how the arts feed our souls. You believe in the power of beauty and the power of a story. You support theaters, art galleries, dance companies and all forms of educational arts outreach.

♎

You bring poise and balance.

Libra is the sign at the middle of the zodiac. It embodies balance. You will always right the scales. You know how to say just the right thing to set things right. Others look to you for your grace and equilibrium. You are compassionately detached.

♎︎

You are even-tempered.

You generally bring a middle-ground to any heightened emotional exchange, dear Libra. You are able to detach and explore the polarities. You bring a desire to bridge the extremes. You are even-keeled.

You connect with loving-intelligence.

In your heart of hearts, you want to engage, play together, cooperate and understand one another deeply. You work to see another's point of view. You open to understand another's pain.

♎

You know how to mediate fairly.

You are a good judge, dear Libra. You listen, assess and weigh. You want the best for both parties. You are impartial. You approach conflict with dispassion.

♎

You stand for social justice.

You will always find a good cause. You stand up for those that need your voice. You like to right the wrongs of our society.

♎

You love the good, the true, and the beautiful.

You deeply believe in a better world. You see what is possible and you live according to higher ideals. You invite in a higher, more effective pattern.

♎

You keep your agreements.

You are true to your word. You are clean and clear in your negotiations. You say what you mean and you mean what you say. You show up.

♎

You foster connection.

You introduce people — to other people, new ideas, and possible endeavors. You know that ideas grow best when discussed and exchanged. You don't want to do this alone.

You love the dance
of partnership.

You love to be related. You engage, dance, kiss, and converse. You share your whole heart with the one you love.

♎

You welcome others
to the party.

You are the ultimate host or hostess. Beauty abounds. And conversation is stimulating. You offer culture and connection. We all want to be at your party, dear Libra.

Living Your Libra Love

How are you feeling, dear Libra? Can you sense the potency of your gifts? Do you want to make the very most of this collaborative, balanced energy of Libra? Here are some thoughts about how to live fully into your Libra love and how to nourish your Libra spirit. Consider them little whispered reminders meant to help you THRIVE. Consider them 'action items'— a loving Libran "to-do" list. Consider them invitations to live the in the world of Libran beauty and partnership.

♎

Be an Activist.

Take on a cause. You will always feel better and most like yourself when you step forward to solve a problem in the name of justice.

♎

Stand for Culture.

Visit an art gallery or see a play. Steep in the arts in any way you choose. Artistry and beauty feed you. Invite a date! Then, you'll be doubly Libra and doubly delighted.

♎

Invite collaboration.

It's your favorite way to work so embrace it fully. Who inspires you? Make a list of all the people you'd love to work with some day. And then let that "some day" be now. Who might you invite for coffee and brainstorming?

Date!

If you're already married, date! If you want to find a partner, date! Take your own self on a date! Say yes to all interesting invitations. Enjoy the art of flirtation. Enjoy the exchange of energy. Be delighted with another (or yourself!)

Interview someone you respect.

You love the back and forth. Interview someone for a newsletter, a video offering or for your own edification. Draw out all they have to offer. Reap the benefits of excellent conversation.

♎

Make some introductions.

If you know someone who needs to meet another someone you know, make that introduction! You know people. You know people who need to meet one another. You might even have some super power match making skills. Go for it!

Promote peace.

You have an ability to bring a greater level of calm and objectivity to conflicted situations. Stand as peace. Speak for peace. Work to create a culture of peace.

Throw a party.
Curate the guest list.

Everyone wants to attend Libra's party. It's going to be beautiful and there will always be fascinating people to talk to. So, don't wait another minute. Throw a party. Celebrate beauty and connection.

Make Art

You do have an eye for design. You are good at composing the beautiful. Call upon the Venus in your nature and make a gorgeous meal, design a book cover, knit a sweater, or write a poem.

♎

Cooperate with the Day.

Start each day by saying "I'm off to cooperate with the day." Try it out! It works! Magic happens.

Growing Your Libra Love

Sometimes, dear Libra, we swing too far in one direction and need to invite a balancing energy to set us right. We are all growing and need to address the parts of ourselves that have not developed as fully. The opportunity for Libra is to invite Aries (your opposite sign) into the picture. Here are ways to grow your Libra love to be more bold, initiating and leadership oriented.

Put on your own oxygen mask first.

We've all heard this many times with every flight we take. But this is particularly important for you, dear Libra. You have a tendency to take care of everyone else, sacrificing every last one of your needs until you are totally depleted. First, make sure you are getting the oxygen you need!

♎

Make many small choices.

It's easy to feel overwhelmed by big decisions. And it's also easy to sit on the fence for far too long. Start making smaller choices that lead to the larger ones. For example, decide to research graduate schools before you decide for sure if and where you are going.

Ask Your Own Self about Your Own Feelings.

Do you ever check in with everyone else to see how they are feeling before you decide how YOU are feeling? Try noticing your own needs, feelings and general emotional state before you become too affected by everyone else. You do not have to absorb the emotional state of any other person or in any way diminish your own to keep the peace.

♎

Release yourself from the opinion of others.

It doesn't matter what anyone else thinks. Make up your own mind. Don't wait for validation. Step forth and offer your ideas.

♎

Decide.

Don't wait too long. Don't let the opportunity pass you by. Don't get stuck in the in-between. You can always change your mind. But decide for this moment.

♎︎

Take action.

Call upon Aries to get up and at 'em. Come forth. Act. Be bold. Assert. Don't wait for someone else to take the first step. Take your OWN first step.

♎

Dare to fly solo.

Be your own Amelia Earhart. Choose your ocean and fly across. You can do it. Sometimes even when we love and prefer to do things in partnership, our greatest growth comes when we dare to fly solo.

Questions to Inspire Sharing Your Libra Love

Dear Libra, here are a few questions or prompts that might inspire or clarify your mission. Grab your journal. Write for 15 minutes about each. Read your writings out loud to a friend. Read them out loud for yourself. Let this exploration nourish your Libran ability to bring greater balance and effective choices to your life.

Write yourself a letter
from your soul.
Greet yourself with love.

♎

Ask yourself
"What does my BEST self
have to say to me at this
moment in my life?"

What ONE conversation might I have right now that could spark healing? What might I say?

♎

Let me tell you about one of the great loves in my life...

What is my next most
important choice?

What relationships in my life need work right now? Why do they need work? Is there a similarity amongst them?

Where am I keeping the peace when it really needs to be temporarily disturbed?

♎

Write a love list. Who and what do you love? Make a list of 50! Read it to someone and encourage them to make one of their own and share it with you!

I wish people would
ask me about...

One Last Little Love Note:

Libra, I hope these questions spark new possibility in your life. You have so much to offer, so much to give. And your ability to connect is rare. If you ever need encouragement, just dip into this little book for a reminder of your light.

Now go forth Libra, and do your thing.

The World is Waiting for YOU.

Big love,
Heidi Rose

About the Author.

Heidi grew up with an astrologer father and an architect mother. Her father taught her the zodiac with her ABC's and her mother taught her to love art and appreciate the beauty of the natural world. She likes to call herself a poet with a map of the heavens in her pocket. Her passion is to inspire and encourage us all to be our truest, most authentic, radiant selves using the tools of astrology and poetry.

www.heidirose.com
Instagram @heidiroserobbins